Alfred's Premier Piano Course

Dennis Alexander • Gayle Kowalchyk • E. L. Lancaster • Victoria McArthur • Martha Mier

Theory Book 2A is designed to correlate with Lesson and Performance Books 2A of *Alfred's Premier Piano Course.* When used together, they offer a fully integrated and unparalleled comprehensive approach to piano instruction.

In addition to written theory, unique features of the book include:

- *Fun Zone*—Explore music through written games and puzzles that truly make theory fun!

- *Imagination Station*—Learn to compose and create.

- *Learning Link*—Discover facts related to history, science, and interesting subjects from daily life based on the music and activities in the course.

- *Now Hear This*—Learn how to listen to music through ear training. Most of these exercises should be done in the lesson.

- *Now Play This*—Learn to sight-read music.

The pages in this book are correlated page by page with the material in Lesson Book 2A. They should be assigned according to the instructions in the upper right corner of each page of this book. They may be assigned as review material at any time after the student has passed the designated Lesson Book page.

Edited by Morton Manus

Cover Design by Ted Engelbart
Interior Design by Tom Gerou
Illustrations by Jimmy Holder
Music Engraving by Linda Lusk

Just turn the page to start your exploration of the fascinating world of music theory!

Fun Zone   View from the Top

Play each musical example as you ride
the elevator to the observation deck.
Begin at the bottom of the page.

Learning Link

Elevators *are the most frequently used
form of mass transportation. Crude
elevator-like lifts were used during the
Middle Ages and can be traced back
to the 3rd century B. C. Today, almost
all elevators use microchip-based
equipment and operate automatically.
Over 340,000 elevators in the United
States travel more than 1.5 billion
miles each year.*

4. Play the G 5-finger pattern with LH.

3. Play the G 5-finger pattern with RH.

2. Name and play the 3 Landmark G's. Use *LH finger 2* on each note.

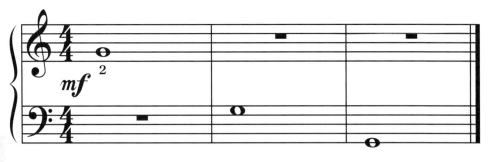

1. Name and play the 3 Landmark C's. Use *RH finger 2* on each note.

Begin
Here

Sharp and Flat Review

1. A sharp sign ♯ raises / lowers a note a half step to the right / left

   (circle one)   (circle one)

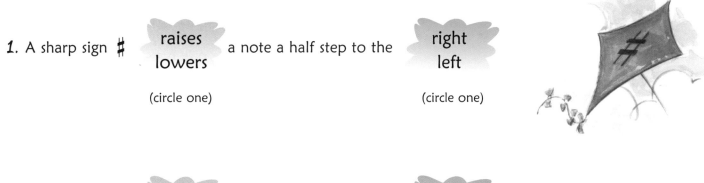

2. A flat sign ♭ raises / lowers a note a half step to the right / left

   (circle one)   (circle one)

3. Name each note. Then play on the keyboard.

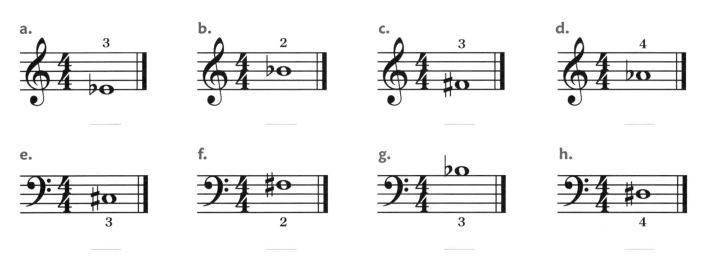

4. **Now Hear This:**

   Circle the pattern that your teacher plays.* Notice the ties.

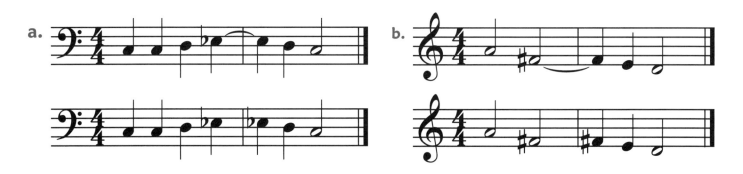

*Note to Teacher:** Play one pattern from each exercise.

C 5-Finger Pattern in Treble Clef

1. Using whole notes, write the C 5-finger pattern *going up*. Name each note.

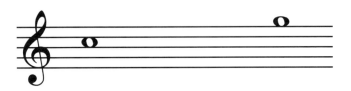

2. Using a whole note, write one note that will make a 3rd between each note. Name the notes.

3. Name each note. Then play on the keyboard.

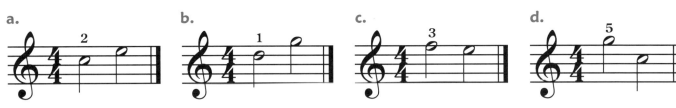

a.   b.   c.   d.

4. Draw a line from each example to the skyscraper with the matching interval name.

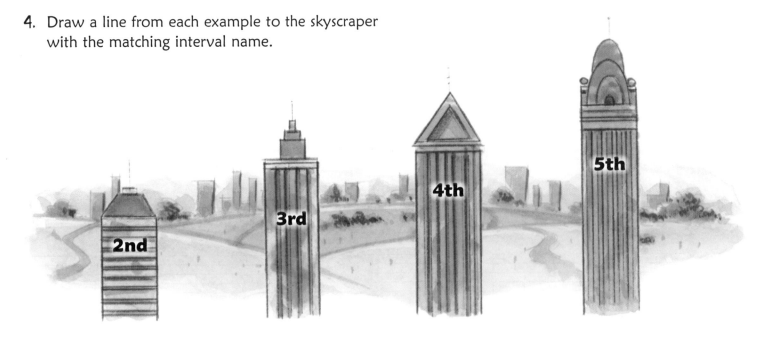

a.   b.   c.   d.

1. **Now Play This:** Draw a flat sign in front of each E.

   Play hands separately first, then hands together.

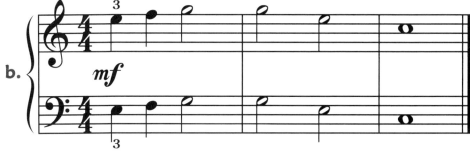

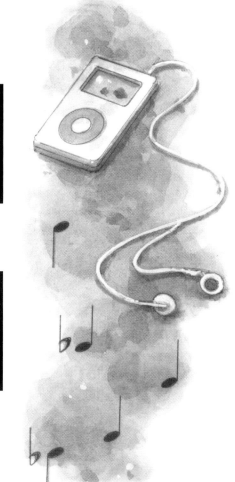

2. **Now Hear This:** Circle the pattern your teacher plays.*

Imagination Station

Add one note under each arrow to complete the melody with notes chosen from the C 5-finger pattern. Write your choices on the staff and then play.

*Note to Teacher:** Play one pattern from each exercise.

6

Crescendo and Diminuendo

1. *Crescendo* means play gradually 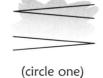 louder / softer

(circle one)

2. *Diminuendo* means play gradually louder / softer

(circle one)

3. Circle the music symbol that matches each term.

a. *Diminuendo*

(circle one)

b. *Crescendo*

(circle one)

4. Draw each music symbol.

a. *Diminuendo*

b. *Crescendo*

Imagination Station

Circle the music symbol that matches the words.

a. Train gets closer.   (circle one)

b. Voices fade away.

c. Thunderstorm approaches.

d. Airplane flies away.

Fun Zone   Jazz Band Drummer

1. Play the drums in the jazz band by tapping each rhythm on the closed keyboard cover. Count aloud.

a.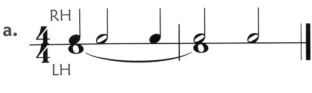

b.

c.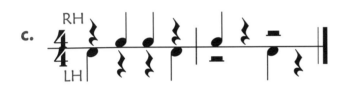

Learning Link

*Big **jazz bands** became very popular starting in the 1920s. These bands often had 10 or more members who played three groups of instruments—brass, woodwinds and rhythm. The brass instruments were almost always trumpets and trombones. Saxophones were the most common woodwind instruments, but clarinets were also included. The rhythm instruments included piano, stringed bass, drums or guitar. The invention of the microphone made it possible to include singers, since now they could be heard over the band instruments.*

2. Fill in the blanks to complete the sentences. Choose your answers from the following words: *Italian, time, fast, tempo.*

a. The _____ is the speed of the beats in a piece of music.

b. Tempo markings are written above the _____ signature.

c. Tempo markings are often written in the _____ language.

d. *Allegro* means _____ or quickly.

3. **Now Play This:** Play and count aloud.

Keep your eyes on the music.

a.

b.

8

Tonic (I) and Dominant (V)
of the C 5-finger Pattern

1. Draw a line from each item in the left column
   to its match in the right column.

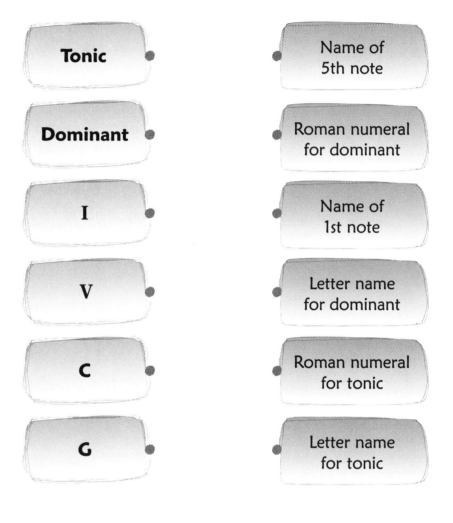

Tonic	Name of 5th note
Dominant	Roman numeral for dominant
I	Name of 1st note
V	Letter name for dominant
C	Roman numeral for tonic
G	Letter name for tonic

Learning Link

Cornelius Gurlitt (1820–1901) was a German pianist, organist and teacher. He studied in Copenhagen, Denmark, and later taught in Hamburg, Germany. He is best known as a composer of over 250 works. Many of his short piano pieces continue to be played today. Enjoy performing the Gurlitt piece on page 12 of Lesson Book 2A.

2. Using a half note, write the dominant note for each tonic note.
   Then write the names of the notes.

a. b. c.

3. Circle each *tonic* note of the C 5-finger pattern. Then draw
   a box around each *dominant* note in the C 5-finger pattern.

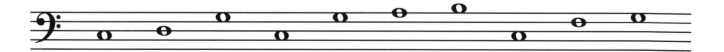

Fun Zone Under the Microscope

Examine the music to answer the questions. Then play and count aloud.

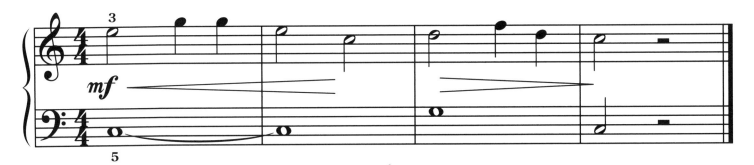

a. What is the name of the first note in the RH? _____

b. Is the first note in the LH **I** or **V**? _____

c. Do measures 1–2 get gradually louder or softer? _____

d. Which LH measure has a dominant note? _____

e. What finger plays the LH note in measure 3? _____

Learning Link

Microscopes are used to make small objects look larger. They are especially useful to scientists. During the 1st century, the Romans discovered that a lens that was thick in the middle and thin on the edges made an object look larger. The first useful microscope was probably developed in the Netherlands around the year 1600. Today, most microscopes are made in Germany, Japan and China and quality microscopes are affordable for almost everyone.

Imagination Station

Using a dotted half note, write a tonic or dominant note in the last two measures. Then play and count aloud.

Tips for Choosing the Correct Note

Use **tonic** when most of the melody notes in the measure are:

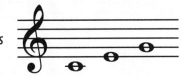

Use **dominant** when most of the melody notes in the measure are:

Accent Sign

1. Draw an accent sign *under* (![accent]) beat 1 of each measure. Then play each rhythm pattern using the note and finger shown on the right. Count aloud.

2. Draw an accent sign *over* (![accent]) beat 2 of each measure. Then play each rhythm pattern using the note and finger shown on the right. Count aloud.

3. **Now Hear This:** Your teacher will play one accent in each pattern.* Draw the accent sign above the correct note.

a.

b.

4. **Rhythm Review:** Tap hands together and count aloud each rhythm pattern. Then tap and say the words.

a.

ham - bur - ger

c.

choc - o - late   cake

b.

chil - i   dog

d.

crisp po - ta - to   chips

*Note to Teacher:** Play one accent in each exercise.

The I Chord

in the C 5-finger Pattern

The **I** chord is formed from the 1st, 3rd and 5th notes in the C 5-finger pattern.
It gets its letter name (C chord) from the bottom note.

1. In each C 5-finger pattern, circle the notes that are used in the **I** (C) chord.

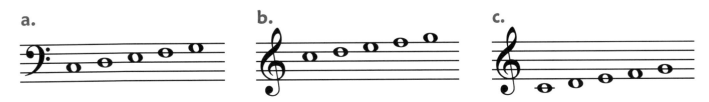

2. Darken the bottom note of each chord. Then circle each **I** (C) chord.

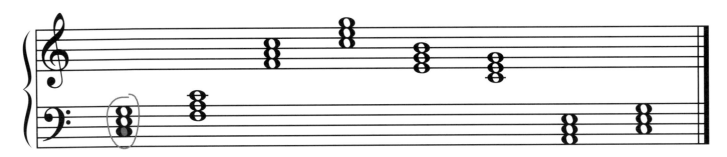

3. Write a whole note to make each example a C block chord.

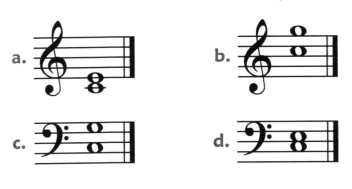

4. Write a whole note in the box to make each example
a C broken chord.

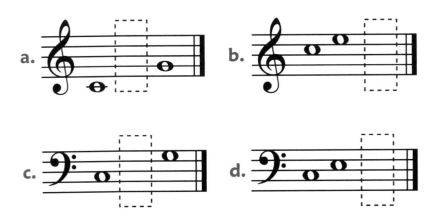

Fun Zone

Learn about the **I** chord in the C 5-finger pattern by riding the Boogie Boards.

1. Play.

2. Write the other two notes of the C broken chord. Use quarter notes.

3. Name the notes.

4. Name the notes.

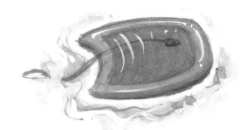

5. Play.

6. Write a whole note to complete the C chord.

The V⁷ Chord
in the C 5-finger Pattern

The **V⁷** chord (**G–B–D–F**) is built on the **5th** note (dominant) of the C 5-finger pattern.

An easy way to get a **V⁷** chord sound is to play the 4th and 5th notes
in the C 5-finger pattern as a 2nd.

1. In each C 5-finger pattern, circle the two notes that are used for the two-note **V7**.

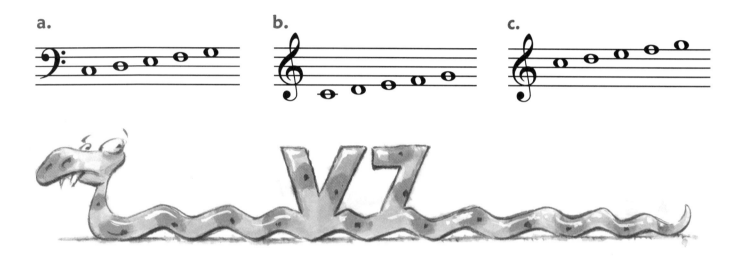

2. Circle each **V7**.

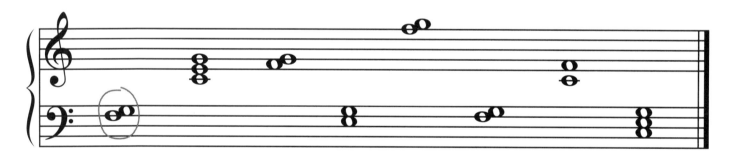

3. Write **I** or **V⁷** on each blank line. Then play and count aloud.

Dynamic Sign—*mp*

1. *mp* means to play moderately _____ .

2. *mp* is [louder / softer] than *p*.

(circle one)

3. *mp* is [louder / softer] than *mf*.

(circle one)

Learning Link

Skate shoes are athletic shoes that have a large, hard plastic wheel built into each heel. People who wear them can switch from walking to rolling on the wheels (called "heeling") by lifting their toes and riding on the heel wheels. One of the most popular brands of skate shoes, called Heelys, was invented by Roger Adams in 2000. Many complicated and daring tricks can be done on skate shoes, making it among the small number of "extreme sports."

4. Using the rhythm shown above the staff, write **I** or **V7** block chords on the staff. Then play and count aloud.

5. Now Hear This: Circle the pattern that your teacher plays.*

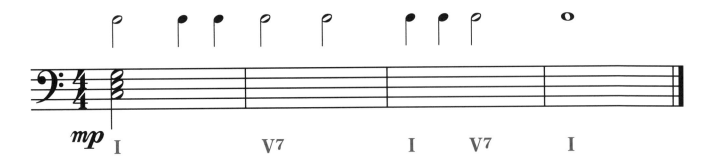

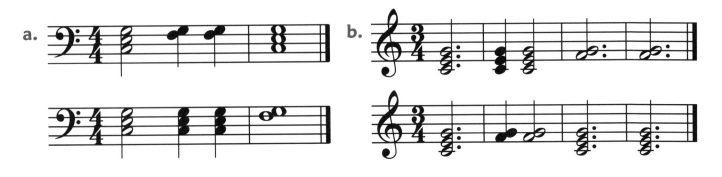

*****Note to Teacher:** Play one pattern from each exercise.

The I and V⁷ Chord

in the C 5-finger Pattern

1. **Moderato** means to play at a _____ tempo.

2. **Now Play This:** Play and count aloud.

Imagination Station

*You have been hired by a famous composer to help finish a piece of music. Write **I** or **V⁷** on the blank line for the correct LH chord in each measure. Then play and count aloud.*

Tips for Choosing the Correct Chord

Use **I** when most of the melody notes in the measure are:

Use **V⁷** when most of the melody notes in the measure are:

16

Eighth Notes

Eighth notes are grouped together in twos or fours. They are joined by a beam.

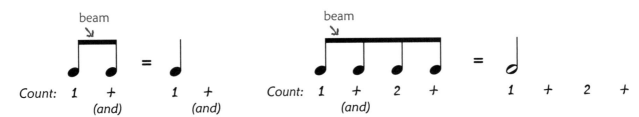

1. Trace the beam for the first pair of eighth notes in each group. Then change
   the quarter notes to eighth notes by adding a beam to each group of two.

2. Trace the beam for the first four eighth notes in each group. Then change
   the quarter notes to eighth notes by adding a beam to each group of four.

3. Draw a line from the quarter-note box on the left to the eighth-note box
   on the right with the same number of beats.

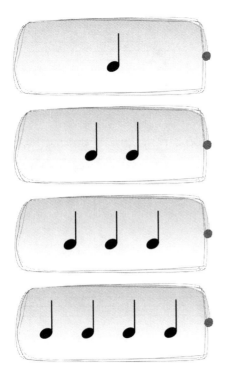
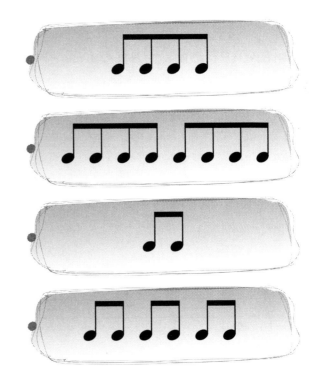

Fun Zone After-School Activities

1. Tap and count each rhythm pattern hands together. Then tap and say the words.

a. school team soc - cer prac - tice

b. do - ing my home - work

c. help with the laun - dry

d. lis - t'ning to my C D's

e. walk the dog

f. watch - ing T. V.

g. play bas - ket ball

h. shop - ping at the mall

2. Write the counts below each rhythm.
Then tap and count aloud.

a.

1 + 2 + 3 +

b.

Learning Link

The computer keyboard is copied from the typewriter keyboard, invented in the 1860s by C. L. Scholes. Originally, the keys were arranged in alphabetical order. However, if one typed too quickly on the earliest typewriter, keys jammed. Because of this, Scholes rearranged the keys so that commonly-used letters of the alphabet were not beside each other. This kept the keys from jamming. The first six keys of the top row of letters on the computer keyboard spell **QWERTY,** *just like this early typewriter.*

Lesson Book: pages 22–23

More About Eighth Notes

1. Balance the bar bells by writing eighth notes (♪♪)
   on the right to match the quarter notes on the left.

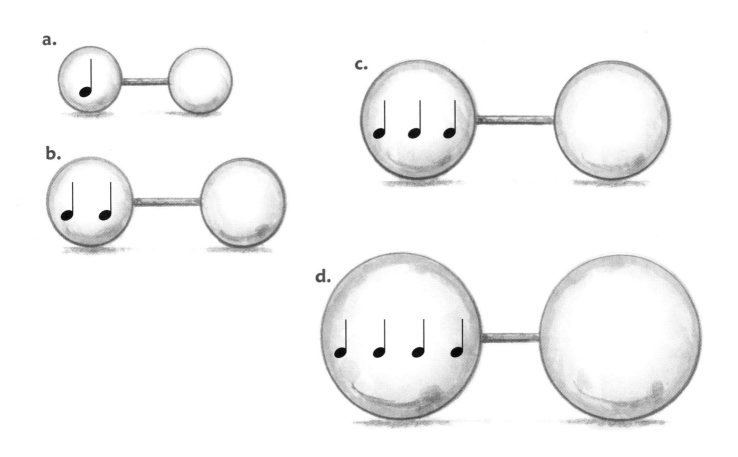

2. **Now Play This:** Play and count aloud.

Fun Zone The Case of the Missing Bar Lines

1. Someone has stolen 9 valuable bar lines and you have found them. Return them by writing them in their correct places in the rhythm patterns below. Notice the time signatures.

2. In each box, add eighth notes to complete each measure with the correct number of beats. Notice the time signatures. Then tap with RH and count aloud.

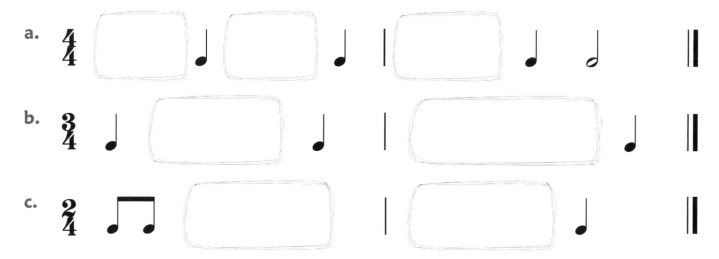

3. **Rhythm Addition:** Add the counts. (♩ = 1 count)

a. ♫ + ♫ + ♩ = 3

b. o + ♩ + ♫ =

c. ♫♫ + ♩ + ♩. =

8va Lower

1. Write an 8va *below* the second note of each example.
   Then play.

2. **Now Hear This:** Circle the rhythm that your teacher taps or claps.*

3. Draw eighth notes to fill each measure.

a.

b.

c.

Learning Link

Traditional music that is passed down from one generation to the next is sometimes described as **folk music.** *Most countries and sometimes regions within a country have distinctive folk music. Some folk music is learned by ear—older people sing and play it so younger generations can copy it without reading music. Examples of folk music are the bush ballads of Australia, the pansori of Korea, the flamencos of Spain, as well as bluegrass music and jazz of the United States.*

*Note to Teacher: Tap or clap one pattern from each exercise.

Natural Sign

The inside square of each natural sign is **on** a line or **in** a space.

line   space

1. Trace the natural sign on line 1. Then draw natural signs *on* the other lines.

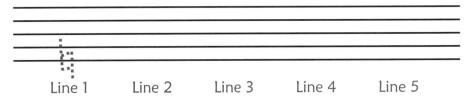

Line 1   Line 2   Line 3   Line 4   Line 5

2. Trace the natural sign in space 1. Then draw natural signs *in* the other spaces.

Space 1   Space 2   Space 3   Space 4

3. A natural is lower / higher than a sharp.

(circle one)

4. On the keyboard, write the names of the natural keys for the labeled sharp keys.

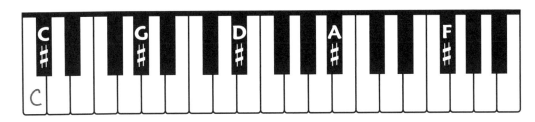

5. A natural is lower / higher than a flat.

(circle one)

6. On the keyboard, write the names of the natural keys for the labeled flat keys.

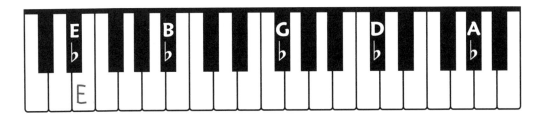

22

Lesson Book: page 27

Fun Zone Under the Microscope

1. Examine the music to answer the questions.
   Then play and count aloud.

Moderato

- **a.** How many natural signs are found in the music? _____ Circle them.
- **b.** What are the two notes played by finger 2? _____
- **c.** What are the two notes played by finger 4? _____
- **d.** In what measure does the music begin to get gradually slower and softer? _____
- **e.** What is the tempo marking? _____

2. Draw a natural sign in front of the second note in each example
   to cancel the sharp or flat. Then name and play the notes.

3. **Now Hear This:** Circle the pattern that your teacher plays.*

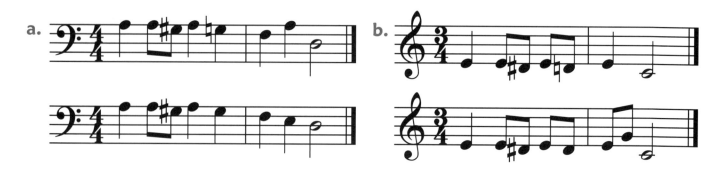

*Note to Teacher: Play one pattern from each exercise.

Fun Zone Terms and Symbols Review

Draw a line from each CD to its matching case.

Lesson Book: page 28

Tonic (I) and Dominant (V)

of the G 5-finger Pattern

Each note of the 5-finger pattern has a name and a number, usually written as a Roman numeral.

Two of the most important notes are:

Note	Roman Numeral	Name
1st note (G)	**I** (1)	Tonic
5th note (D)	**V** (5)	Dominant

G 5-finger Pattern

1st note   5th note

G   D

I   V

Tonic   Dominant

1. Circle the correct answer for each statement below.

a. Tonic is the name of the 1st / 5th note in the G 5-finger pattern.

b. **V** is the Roman numeral for tonic / dominant

c. **I** is the Roman numeral for tonic / dominant

d. D is the letter name for the tonic / dominant note in the G 5-finger pattern.

2. Circle each tonic note in the G 5-finger pattern.
Then draw a box around each dominant note in the G 5-finger pattern.
Remember: The dominant note can be written *higher* or *lower* than tonic.

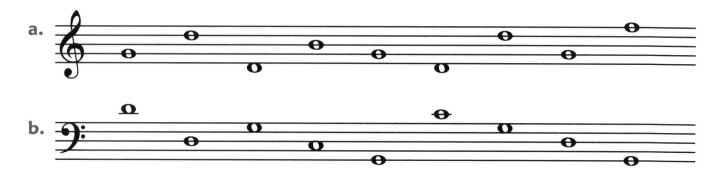

a.

b.

The I and V⁷ Chords

in the G 5-finger Pattern

The **I** chord is formed from the 1st, 3rd and 5th notes in
the G 5-finger pattern. It gets its letter name (G chord)
from the bottom note.

1. In each G 5-finger pattern, circle the notes that are used in the **I** (G) chord.

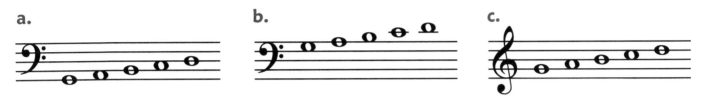

2. Darken the bottom note of each chord. Then circle each **I** (G) chord.

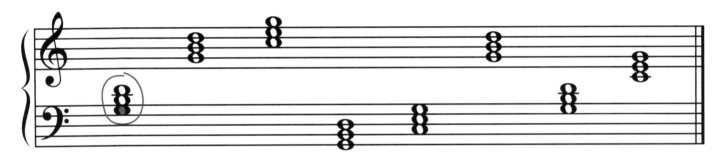

The **V7** chord (**D**–F♯–A–C) is built on the **5th** note (dominant) of the G 5-finger pattern.

An easy way to get a **V7** chord sound is to play the 4th and 5th notes
in the G 5-finger pattern as a 2nd.

3. In each G 5-finger pattern, circle the two notes that are used for the two-note **V7**.

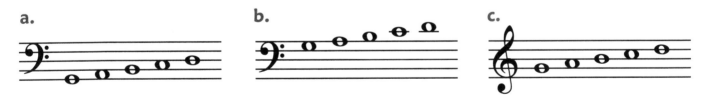

4. Circle each **V7**.

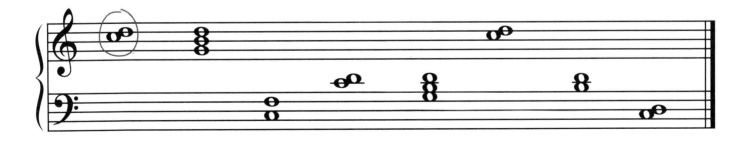

More About the I and V7 Chords

in the G 5-finger Pattern

Lesson Book: pages 30–31

1. Write **I** or **V7** on the blank line. Then play and count aloud.

2. Using the rhythm shown above the staff, write **I** and **V7** block chords on the staff.
Then play and count aloud.

3. Now Hear This: Circle the pattern that your
teacher plays.*

Learning Link

*The **Tilt-A-Whirl**, a popular carnival ride, was invented by Herbert Sellner in 1926 and first operated in an amusement park in Minnesota. Today, Tilt-A-Whirls usually have seven cars that can spin in one direction, then another. The fun builds as the car spins, hesitates, then swings quickly in the other direction. The spinning movement of each car depends on the weight of its passengers and where they sit in the car. It is impossible to predict how a car will move during the ride!*

*Note to Teacher: Play one pattern from each exercise.

Pedal Sign

1. **Now Play This:** Play and count aloud. Notice the pedal sign.

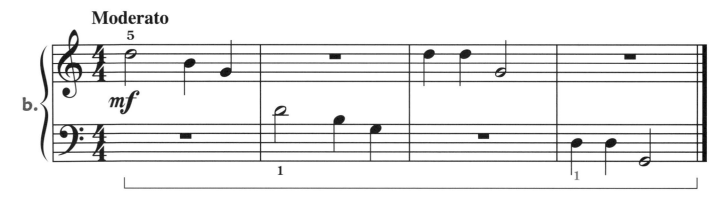

2. Draw a line to connect each tempo term to its meaning.

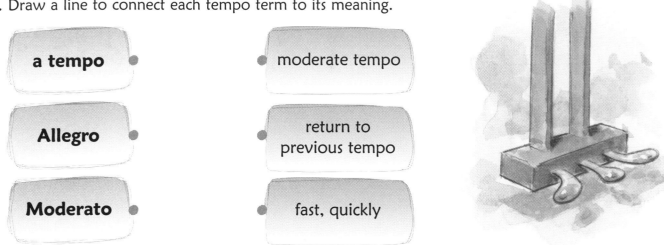

a tempo

Allegro

Moderato

moderate tempo

return to previous tempo

fast, quickly

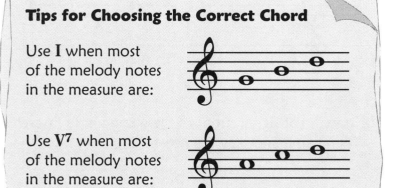

Tips for Choosing the Correct Chord

Use **I** when most of the melody notes in the measure are:

Use **V⁷** when most of the melody notes in the measure are:

Imagination Station

Write **I** *or* **V⁷** *on the blank line for the correct LH chord in each measure. Then play and count aloud.*

Moderato

Half Steps

1. On the keyboard, write H on the key that is a half step *higher* than the labeled key.
Then write L on the key that is a half step *lower*.

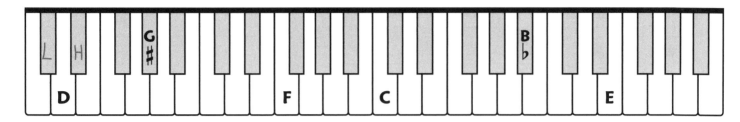

2. Circle the half steps. Then play each example.

3. Draw a sharp sign in front of the *second* note in each example to make a half step *higher*.
Then name and play the notes.

4. Draw a flat sign in front of the *second* note in each example to make a half step *lower*.
Then name and play the notes.

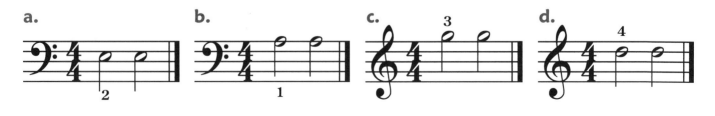

Fun Zone What's Wrong with the Computer?

The computer music program is printing things incorrectly!
Check each example, decide what is wrong, then write it correctly.

What's Wrong?	Fix It!
1. **I** in the C 5-finger Pattern	**I** in the C 5-finger Pattern
2. **V7** in the G 5-finger Pattern	**V7** in the G 5-finger Pattern
3.	
4. C♯ is the same key as D♯.	C♯ is the same key as ____ .
5. G♭ is the same key as F♮.	G♭ is the same key as ____ .
6. Allegro means play slowly.	Allegro means play ____ .

Whole Steps

1. On the keyboard, write H on the key that is a whole step *higher* than the labeled key.
Then write L on the key that is a whole step *lower*.

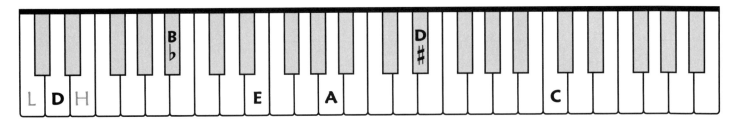

2. Circle the whole steps. Then play each example.

3. Using half notes, write the note that is a whole step *higher* than each given note.
Use sharps for black keys. Then name and play the notes.

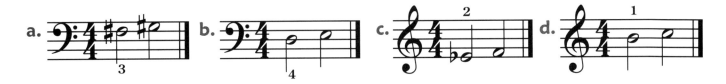

4. Using half notes, write the note that is a whole step *lower* than each given note.
Use flats for black keys. Then name and play the notes.

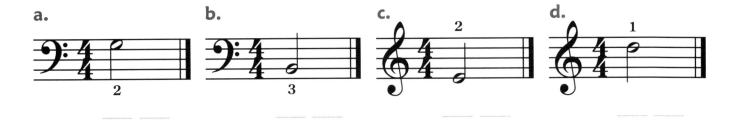

Fun Zone Beat the Clock!

How quickly can you answer these questions? Ask an adult or another student to time you.

Learning Link

People first told time by looking at the sun as it crossed the sky. The oldest actual **clock** was the sundial, invented about 5,500 years ago. The first reliable pendulum clock was invented by Christian Huygens about 1655. In the 20th century, electric clocks became popular. The most accurate clocks are atomic ones that measure time to the billionth of a second.

Say the letter name of the chord. Then play.

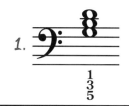

Say the Roman numeral name of the chord in the C 5-finger pattern. Then play.

Name and play the note. Then name and play the note a whole step higher.

Name and play the note.

Name and play the interval.

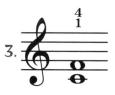

Name and play the note. Then name and play the note a half step lower.

Total Time: _____ minutes

_____ seconds

The C Major and G Major 5-Finger Patterns

1. Circle the row of chocolates that has the correct order of whole (W) and half (H) steps for a major 5-finger pattern.

2. Complete the major 5-finger patterns by drawing notes in the boxes. Circle each half step. Then write **I** under each tonic note and **V** under each dominant note.

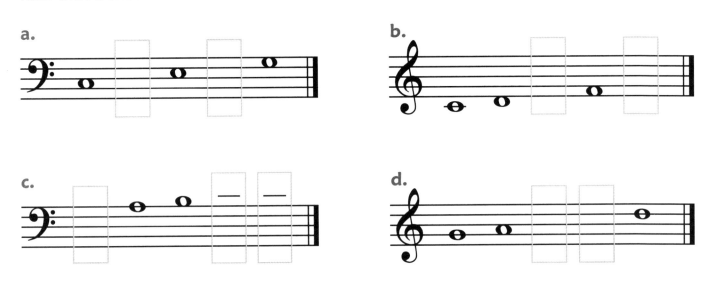

3. Draw a line from each half or whole step example to its matching name.

Whole Step

Half Step

The D Major and A Major 5-Finger Patterns

1. Complete the major 5-finger patterns by writing notes in the boxes. Circle each half step. Then write **I** under each tonic note and **V** under each dominant note.

a.

b.
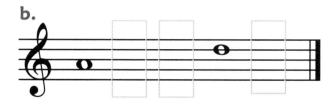

c.

d.
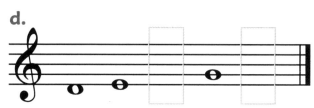

2. Name the sharp in the D major 5-finger pattern. ____

3. Name the sharp in the A major 5-finger pattern. ____

4. **Now Play This:** On the line *above* each staff, write the name of the 5-finger pattern. Then play and count aloud.

a. _____ Major 5-finger Pattern

b. _____ Major 5-finger Pattern

c. _____ Major 5-finger Pattern

34

The I and V⁷ Chords
in the D Major 5-finger Pattern

1. Write **I** or **V⁷** on the blank line. Then play and count aloud.

2. Using the rhythm shown above the staff, write **I** and **V⁷** block chords on the staff.
Then play and count aloud.

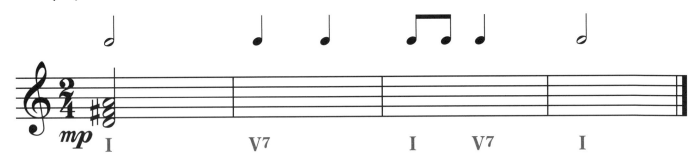

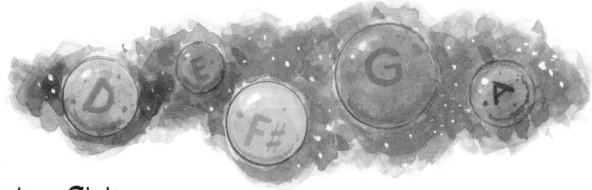

Imagination Station

Using this rhythm, make up a RH melody with notes from the
D major 5-finger pattern. Begin and end with D.

Fun Zone Transposition Party

On the lines below the staff in the middle, write the name of each interval.
Circle *up* or *down* for the interval direction. Then draw a line from the
middle staff to the staff on the right or left with the correct transposition.

a.

_____ _____ _____
up   up   up
down down down

b.

_____ _____ _____
up   up   up
down down down

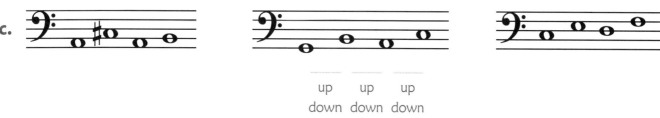

c.

_____ _____ _____
up   up   up
down down down

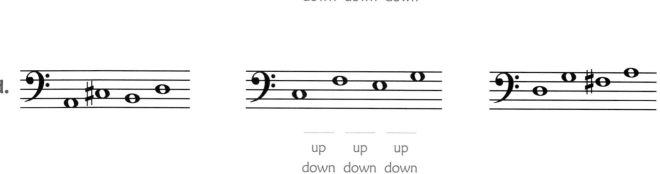

d.

_____ _____ _____
up   up   up
down down down

6ths

Lesson Book: page 42

1. Write the alphabet letter that is *up* a 6th.

a. C  **b.**  **c.**  **d.**

E   G   D   B

2. Write the alphabet letter that is *down* a 6th.

a. C **b.** G **c.** A **d.** F

3. Draw a ✓ under all the 6ths on the staffs and keyboards.
Write the name of the interval under the others.

 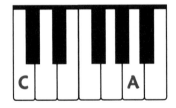 

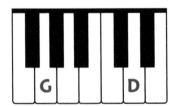  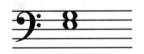 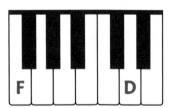

 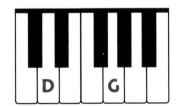 

More About 6ths

1. Circle the melodic and harmonic 6ths in the music. Then play and count aloud.

How many 6ths did you circle? _____

How many 6ths did you circle? _____

2. Using a quarter note, write each melodic interval *up* and *down* from E.
Remember: Stems *down* if the notehead is on line 3 or above.
Stems *up* if the notehead is below line 3.

3. Now Hear This: Your teacher will play a 3rd or 6th.*

Circle the interval that you hear.

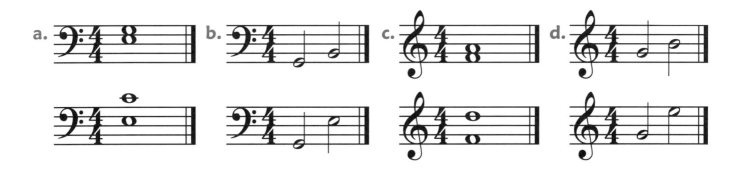

***Note to Teacher:** Play one interval from each exercise.

Lesson Book: pages 44–45

Fun Zone   The Sports Page

The *Musical Times* newspaper has a new sports writer. You can read his article about an exciting baseball game by naming the intervals, filling in the blanks and completing the rhythm addition.

Learning Link

Newspapers were originally simple handwritten notices posted in public places as early as 59 B.C. in ancient Rome. The first regularly published newspaper began in Germany in 1609. Today, most newspapers use computers to lay out and design the printed pages. Some people even prefer to read their daily newspaper on the computer. Although news is also available on television and radio, written news is almost always more complete.

Last night's baseball game between the All Stars and the Super Stars was an exciting one! The

All Stars were up to bat first. The first player made it to 𝄢 **8** base. The

(name interval)

batter made it to 𝄢 base. The bases were loaded after the 𝄞 batter hit

a ground ball and was safe at first base. The 𝄢 batter hit a home run! By the bottom

of the 𝄞 inning, the score was tied _____ to _____ .

(add number of counts)

It was the Super Stars' turn to bat. They had two outs. Everyone was hoping that there wouldn't

be a  out. The pitcher threw a _____ ball. The batter swung. The ball
(Allegro)

went out of the park! The crowd was on their feet as the Super Stars scored their

run of the evening! In the _____ inning, it suddenly started to rain. The game was

called, and the crowd quickly left the stadium. The final score was:

Super Stars _____ , All Stars _____ .

Fun Zone Dragon Hunt

Help the knight find the dragon by removing the obstacles in his path.
Put an X through each *incorrect* example as you follow the dragon's trail.

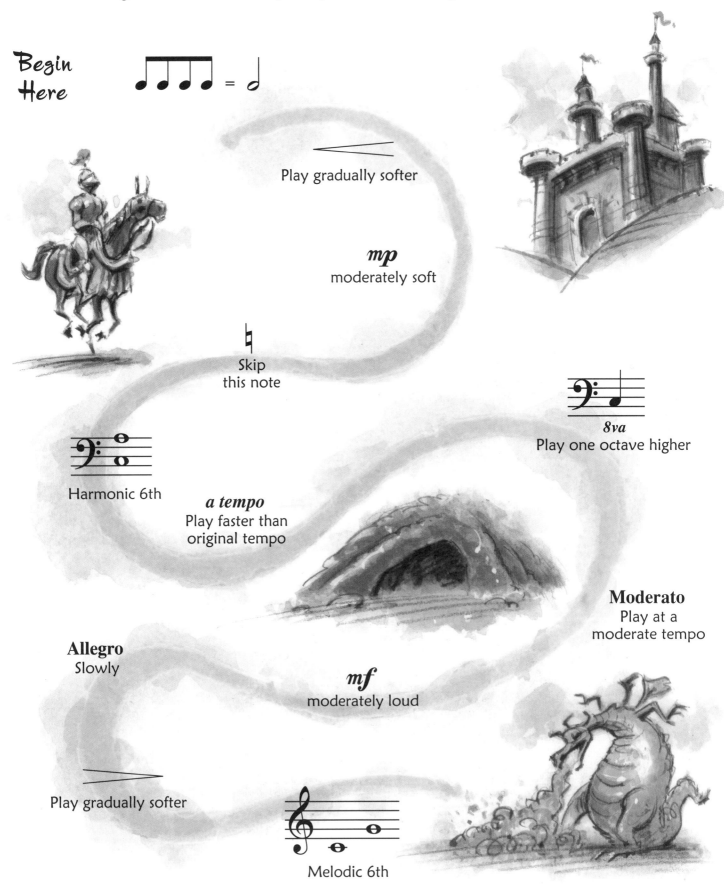

Begin Here

♩♩♩♩ = 𝅗𝅥

Play gradually softer

mp
moderately soft

Skip
this note

8va
Play one octave higher

Harmonic 6th

a tempo
Play faster than
original tempo

Moderato
Play at a
moderate tempo

Allegro
Slowly

mf
moderately loud

Play gradually softer

Melodic 6th